Peter Naumann

WINTER COUNT

STARBORN BOOKS

Peter Naumann

WINTER COUNT
by Peter Naumann

First published in 2013
by Starborn Books
Wales, U.K.

e-mail: sales@starbornbooks.co.uk
website: www.starbornbooks.co.uk

This is No. ....133.. of a limited
signed First Edition of 150 copies

Printed and bound in the UK by Berforts Information Press, Hertfordshire

ISBN 978 1 899530 48 9

Dust jacket painting by Anuk Naumann

CONTENTS

Acknowledgements

My thanks go first of all and most of all to Peter Oram, without whom this book would not have come about; to my family for their unfailing support and enthusiasm (with special thanks to my mother for the cover image); to Josh Warren for telling me the story which lies at the bottom of 'Guests' (below many fathoms of misremembering on my part); to Misha Herwin, Conny Lippert, Anna Godfrey, Josh Adcock, and Michael Malay, and to my fellow participants in the Bristol Poetry Institute's creative writing workshop in February-March 2013, led by Rachael Boast, for their stimulating comments on the poems at various stages of their production; to John McGuirk, Janie Hextall, Tina Burnett, Ika Willis, Chris Roaf, Steven Lovatt, Naomi Pendle, Chris Mason, Anna Pearson, Ed Targett, Andy Wormald, and many other friends with whom I have discussed poetry and poetics over the last few years, and whose insights have altered and enriched my understanding of what I am doing as a writer; and to the staff of Bristol University Library and Oxfordshire County Libraries, where, in the course of much aimless meandering (and the occasional focussed foray), I followed many of the threads which contribute to the fabric of this book.

'Retreat' and an earlier version of 'Seen in Passing, Cycling North' were first published in *Helicon* (Winter 2012-13); 'Algebra', and alternative versions of 'Winter Count' and 'Orlebar Variations' were exhibited at the Parlour Showrooms, Bristol, as part of Bristol Arts-week in February 2013.

For my family, for Holly, and for
all friends, north and south of the river

WINTER COUNT

mind unshod
still leaves
vestiges in sand,
crossing parchment

(after Sappho and Anne Carson)

Fayyum

i.

decade in and decade
out, century
after century, you wake:

always the press of linen
on your eyes and lips, always
some new murmur of a south
wind in the air,
unsettling the tethered ships

~

by such sounds as reach
you, their muffled but familiar
clank and chatter, you would think

the clockhands must have stalled,

or a crumb of mica, maybe,

lodged

in the straits of the hourglass, had

silted the passages past navigation,

choking the commerce of its hemispheres —

for surely the same chandlers come and go

between the wharves and drydock?

surely

the same hempworkers, caulking

crews and galleyhands

scramble and gossip, swap

the same jokes and compare the selfsame

scars and bruises, betting on tribunal

elections, mooting weather's

whims in Punic or Minoan *koiné*,

Demotic barbed with Hyksos slang?

(and who can count those, one day to go

down, tipped from scaffolding or rotten

ladders

into dark

fathoms, where the great

fish eat them bone by bone ...)

~

nothing new, then, under this

instalment of the sun — or so

your ears might have you reason,

but in wynds and alleyways, below the radar's

fingers, fabric, lapis and enamel

for unforeseen, unprecedented

flags and brooches do

the rounds, accruing

acreage and lustre with each

handling, passing-on and turning over

ii.

so another season's vigil passes, attentive

to the dial

every inch and minute of the night,

following,

with azimuth and alidade, the arc

of seconds

at their stations, indefatigable

hours shuttling

west or riding

north on the trail of truant

comets — tailing, never

gaining, on the spent,

absconding constellations;

stars and passengers together

going feral — further,

fierier and faster with each latitude

GUESTS

All morning watching

Weather as if

From an abandoned firespotter's

Cabin in Hokkaido — coffee, haiku,

Ainu bells, eleven

Inches of new snow

~

Come noon, visitors,

Prompt as ever:

First, the novice in a thousand

Pieces, who forgot to write

Stanzas of the Heart

Sutra on his arms, legs,

Face and forehead,

Every hair and last

Disputed

Reach of skin; close

After him, nose ripped

Away and leaving

Only a tremor's weal, one

Who

     did not

          nor ever

Now is likely to

        forget

RETREAT

From this point you find

Only stone, stolen

Rivers, and whatever

Shapes the wind can hazard

Given gold and silica and seven

Times however

Many years you had in mind

~

        As for all the best

Occasions, wear the same

Green as the country left

Behind, head bared, so

As to make certain

This is snow —

        not tickertape,

Not the memory

Flaking out or frosting over

GILA

Plants and painted stones insist

On their proper names, no less

Their allegories — *African Rue, American*

Plum, Beautiful

Fleabane, Bitter Cherry — outcasts

At my heels

With a petition,

A dossier of grievances

Exacted by a scorpion's pin,

Aimed at the sweet and narrow

Place between the sky and outer skin.

PILOT

'You'll know you must be getting near
When the first snakes appear,

Black about the head or gold
All over, another waver

Perplexing lines of water;
But remember, better

Gifts will follow — malabathrum,
Peacocks and long pepper,

Cinnamon, skins
Shrunk and ravelled,

         staples,

Luxuries and baubles, each
A glint of what maybe

Lies over the horizon,

Where the land you hear

Described as Sind or Hind,

Ceylon or serendipity

                        (depending

Who you ask and how

Their tongues translate)

Dwindles at a constant rate

Toward the rest of our red

Ocean, ruled and robbed

From this end to the further

Shore by varied kings and sundry

Villains in their glad and gloomy habits.'

GOODNIGHT-LOVING TRAIL

Keep charcoal and plenty

Tins on hand,

In case you need to make a casket:

Hammer them thin

As your mallet can

                   handle, so

The cries of one

Not quite so dead as you had reckoned

When you went over him with mirror,

Match and needle might yet reach you

Through the huff and trample and tirade

Of ninety thousand

Steers, north of recommended grass.

PROGRESS

i.

Where Goethe goes, fire follows —

    Ilmenau,

        Tiefurt,

            Stützebach —

                nights kindle

Accustomed mischief

In starved grass, the west wind cannot leave

Cinders to themselves, while hay remains

As liable as ever, even

In these damp and orderly domains,

This enlightened eighteenth century of ours.

ii.

Again the moon, sharpener of moleboards,

In my mind and eastward,

Leaves the tethers of the west behind,

A headstrong fruit eloping from her rind;

Prized and promised in each nick of water,

Delayed by ploughs' and any other's share,

Misled by herring, busying

Eels and sleight

Of hand, at last

She makes it

To her winter camp without an ounce to spare.

SEEN IN PASSING, CYCLING NORTH

discarded rubber tubing, roofing felt,
plywood, fujifilm (september
lapping many colours, wilting
tesserae to sepia);

sideroads;

snakes alive and dead and undecided;

damsontrees and dodder, tares and wheat;

eight fields of oilseed, each a home or brief
retreat for guinea
                        fowl and partridge, straining
eyes to tell the buzzard's
shadow from the ruses of the sun;

cows — stoical,

peripatetic,

pythagorean;

imperceptible

changes in the curvature

of earth, with all

the little lazy tilts

you'd never guess your body

made or might

discover once again

GAZETTEER

i.

      Reading *Onomasticon,* the first image
In your mind is a dewlapped, sweaty
Beast, all tusks and blubber, unexpected
Bouts of speed —

                Odontotyrannus, Fastitocalon —
Fanged usurper, gnashing

                          despot, or
A nightmare prompted by the sleek
Motions as a school of tunny

        surge and plummet in dark water;

      Opening the cover, yellowed cities
Spill across the arid sheets and spell
Themselves, a primer of dilapidated
Domes and palisades — Pataliputra,
Chorazin, Bethsaida, Al-
Taj, each with its complementary

Larks and lesions where the waters came,

Collected, failed and faded,

Into earth and out of anybody's hands.

ii.

I dry my hair by poring over

Maps of sparse and scalded

Places — the Sahel and Sahara quick

To act: the Great Sand

Sea, the spidering radius

of 'Uwaynat, Gilf Kebir, Grand

Erg du Djourab, Ennedi effective even

When incongruous in cartographers'

Fatigues, dressed for unassuming

Altitudes as if for champagne

Country, terrain you might imagine

Neither dove nor crow would starve

To cross on their commute between

Wide tropic river and bright slender sea.

iii.

Prospectors by the shipload, headed
For the false and true Horn, taking
The longer, safer passage, south and north
Again to San Francisco, lean
To port and listen
In to Africa below the Happy
Isles, hear only
Voices of a desert, vague with dust,
For in these latitudes, before the Doldrums,
Let alone the Doctor
On her rounds, the Harmattan
Delights to paint all
Passersby with cinnabar,
An embarrassment of paprika
Attested by all hands out walking
On the ropes before the early rain.

~

Splashdown here, titanium

Delayed by silk, and who would doubt

You when they drew

Thumb or finger through the patina of rouge,

Who dispute

Your tale of hazard, narrow

Escape and steep expulsion from the tablelands of Mars,

Loess left unruffled by that nosedive through the stars?

iv.

Mercator so adored the poles, that, compensating

For exaction of his parallels

From points as near as any

To infinity, he granted

Each a double share

In his revised and permanent

Settlement of the squared and quartered circles of the earth;

Thanks, then, to Mercator and the flattened earth he coaxed

To birth, paring and unfurling

Meridians without a tear,

I can crouch within whatever light

                  collects in the corner of a winter

Room and count

Irregularities in the skin of Greenland,

Itemise fjords and basins and the blush

Of lichen

      at the gills as southern coasts regale with thaw;

                      it is enough —

Such vast, albino fruit, entangled

In the upper registers, each nick demanding

Equal purchase on the pristine matter —

To make you

Wonder

If this copy of the world were only

An uncorrected proof, one glaring

           sector waiting to be coloured in.

CAREER

now and then — now, under

wholesale and selected

stars, bespoke and catholic

clothes of night, as then —

        i could be arrested (reeling

to some other room or, half

turned, on haling,

breathless stairs) by any

              sudden, altered

detail in the sway of air,

such as might be set in

train by an apprentice starling,

who that moment learned

           by heart the final

lesson of unwitnessed flight and clapped

together ivy, tapered

wings to prompt the sky's applause

ELEVEN BELOW

Weather worse than this, and Brueghel

The elder would have been abroad,

Given a chance or half

An hour's start,

Togged and happed to the final thread

(Camlet, ermine, fresh and reeking

Woollens, felted clogs you couldn't

                    buy in Antwerp,

Nor in Amsterdam,

For any of your love or lucre),

Cocking every ear for angles

Of the spade, the chime

                    on tarmacadam

Like a far, uncertain flight

Of chantry bells; for asthma

In the breath of infant buildings —

Spindly banisters and crucks

Of barns raised barely

Two weeks back and waiting

On the ice to lick them into trim.

34

Water persists, ruins

                          any machine

                          intent on running

into rivers unprepared.

Weirs superannuate,

                          dilapidate, heap

spools and shallows with ironmongery,

silverware —

                          salvageable, purposes

of algae, schemes

of grass and gravel

                          notwithstanding.

~

Massacres,

          King Phillip's

war and all the others left

metal and more perishable

                          elements to fuse and fail

                  in tandem here, between

incessant humming

                wire and shallows

rich for seining, staked

                  for future acquisitions.

~

Siblings,

        banked, eat bread,

                thistles and brown

sugar on a foot of shingle

            before the reveries resume

their erstwhile and accustomed places —

John engrossed with oar and canvas,

caulking wax and other

tackle, Henry David

                dabbling, counting

relics and remaining rapid fishes.

How fortunate are we, who did not own an acre of these shores... The poor rich man! All he has is what he has bought. What I see is mine. I am a large owner in the Merrimack intervals...

Thoreau, *A Week on the Concord and Merrimack Rivers*

MANNAHATTA

Wait long enough, stay

Still enough, and trees

Will grow on you, sailcloth

Dissipate to Spanish Moss,

Scuttled firetrucks and ferries swarm with coral.

Perhaps in time

                    the albatross, holystoning

Overdue and short

On hemp, will stagger, darned and bleary, back

Toward Elysium, barely

Nodding as she rediscovers

Fresh Kills,

Paterson and Hackensack and Hoboken and tips

Her wings a touch

Further than the headwind bids her

Anyhow to squabbling

Guillemots, convened impromptu

Where contorted, serviceable branches

Break the water — scaffolds of an aspen

Importuned by winters and long waiting.

Lie down in the East

River or any

Other long enough:

Trees will grow on you.

SOUND OF HARRIS

looking at what the sea does

to the west, to what we think

are ships poised

as if

at chosen stages, after

deliberate and measured

pauses, calling

attention to a level

notch of pewter between one

blue, another, and the several

scripts of silver, still

we stretch

our ears for the least

suggestion of aught

invisible, auks or petrels

recounting oceans and their cost,

hear only wind and dwindling

bells and sheep with no illusions

UIG

South and east again, surrounded

By green and rearing spaces,

Rock and sphagnum,

Flags and any

Number of unnoticed faces

~

Perhaps we could, in passing

Try to see this

       landscape

From the corncrake's angle;

       calling ground,

Wind-tilted bush and bound

Beaten to ring with

Bone, comb and the keen

White dash of coral, islands waxing

Full or wasting into water, hidden

In the apron of the ocean, out of hearing

Looking Glass

At the limit of generous land,

Eyes of gravel and gypsum grow

Chary of lashes, moccasin

Leather making

A bid for devolution. Under the same

Sky, the same conditions, he notes

Grasses as the moon,

In the guise of a knife,

Might appraise the qualities of water.

~

'The first time you put a ploughshare in that earth,

It made a sound just like a zipper' — snickering

Through ancient ways and means of grass,

A line of havoc in the earth's securities;

Rhizomes matting to the lope of steel,

Prairie for the first

Time shorn and friable.

ORLEBAR VARIATIONS

i. Branch Line

Between the lurch and stutter, leaving

Redland for Montpelier, you see,

Past willowherb, in yellow trees,

Alone, aloft yet

Slack,

A lantern like a bag of lava,

Souvenir of Chingkangshan.

ii. Grass Roof

Sometimes you are startled

By the sun without

Seeing so much

As a sliver of her colours;

Rather, you

Behold

A clumped and interrupted chain

Of daubs — the rent

Where a screed of sudden, incandescent

                currency was lost

Among the lukewarm clouds.

iii. Case Histories

Behind glass and in the open

Air, where mistletoe suggests

A pterodactyls' eyrie,

Rife with bones, and mazes

Cut in moss repeat

The winding earthward

Plunge of meteors, this city goes

Out of its way in order

To remind you

       of apocalypse; unveiling,

Ring by ring, the teem of forests

Laid down and set aside

Before the axe, errata and anomalies

In Cambrian and prior strata —

Salps and *charnia*, demanding

Glyphs, resistant

To the business of translating

Shales and veins and vanished seas.

iv. Palm Sunday

Count steps, climbing

A city and its stairways, sideways;

Pick cans and candy

Papers from lawn crestfallen

At the summer's haste

To get here; do not be deterred

By the magpie, closest

Approximation

      to Archaeopteryx,

Nor by grey birds arguing

Over a willow or a walnut branch.

v. Poise

Kites flaunt every finger to the last

Flinch of crimson though

As yet the slopes remain

Several tints from auburn,

Flourishing however

Little henna can be gleaned

From bracken's rust and raw

Tobacco before towers

Intervene and dangle

A bridge on chains, a spirit

Level testing out the air for any

Tilt or possibly

     a timepiece, moving

Yet languid to the point of lull;

At any rate, six hundred

     feet of similes

In steel between me and the spare,

Intermittent woodland where

I imagine you

Might walk in such

Sunlight as the mountain

Ash or hazel brakes allow.

vi. Elysium

Through high corn, slanting

Steel, shoulder of a moon

Reformed in metal, interloper

From another river, held

Up for all the world and any

Other like a *thyrsus*

Or a pennant, furled and out

Of favour for a second season.

vii. Motley

At the beeches' feet, their bonnets,

Petite and threadbare

Phrygian caps discarded

47

at the last *journée.*

Come closer, see

How, stubborn in the face of pith

And bark's best efforts

To iron them away, the ragged work

Remains, epigrams

Of bliss, dejection and desire,

Scored and pending

Recompense, dispersed

Petitions for a common wealth.

viii. Tryst

The watch weighs on

My wrist, a needle,

Eager for the north,

The polar

Fells and floes.

       No time

Remains for firewater, talk

Of globes, each with a double

Hide, or dancing, even

Now the tables have been turned

Over and resolved

Into their several

                parts; none

Left to gather,

Fathom or divine

Fleeting, equivocal

Gambits in your eyes — time only

                for the moon to rise,

Stop, stand and stare

At her feet with surprise —

Once nimble as a lariat but now

Fast with frost halfway through winter skies.

ix. Climbing Cabot Tower

The first time, rain, and last
Time, sleet,
Scared east and down the river into snow.

I cannot remember now how hard
I tried to make out
Shapes of streets or houses,
Sift the future's
Sounds between the leaves, before
Losing heart and hearing
                          only autumn's
Plash on gilt or silver, patterns
                          varied in the telling
Details, repetitions
                          notwithstanding, just
Enough to keep my eyes and ears
From isolating frequencies of yew,
Holm, sycamore and ash, accepting
Nothing but the deluge as the true
Gift of the heavens when all's said,

All's done, and this

    long, sodden season's through.

~

We listened past our chattering
Teeth to blizzards

    in the doorway, looking

Out when the swirling
Fit had whispered

    to a hush, to find

Glaciers

    returned and sprawling, seeming

Unbothered by whatever
Brevity of sleep they saw
Ahead.

    So, before they gave

Over their ghosts and gathered
Up their sheets and bits and pieces,
Whether taking notice of the sun's
Injunction or the moon's advice,
We slid away,
Downhill to Park Street on a slick of ice.

EYE OF HORUS

the moth and tutelary god translated

to a blazon, lampblack gives

out, and what the ones who ought

to know continue

calling water stays

rank, illegible

with pesticide and moonlight as before;

dunes contribute the expected

fleet and glancing

metals, unexpected

songs — for nobody

thought to point

out to the jackals,

owls and nightjars where the small

print stipulates, in black and white and words

jealous of syllables if prodigal

with clauses, the discretion,

sepia and silence

enjoined on the supporting

cast and crew and extras in this motion picture

CLIPPINGS

ταν αχειμαντον τε Μεμφιν και δονακωδεα Νειλον

Bacchylides, fr.30 (Athenaeus, *epitom.* 1.36)

Thanks to the occasional rain of Egypt, moths,

Silverfish, and scribal diffidence,

You can tell us little now

But gold and pebbled places'

Inclinations toward gravel,

Toward sand, or how

Thrift, centaury and campion learn

The knack of living

With loopholes when the ocean almost

Overreaches, almost reassures

Itself in fleeting

Pools, salt marsh and meadow,

Machair and what little

Yet remains of wilderness,

Unclaimed or common land.

DIDCOT

An hour and a quarter from the west;

Mercia, the Marches and the rest

A little way

Behind us now, the Andes

Returning in the clothes of clouds ahead:

Towers let off steam, a lucid rhyme

About their motions, time

More even in their music

Than the scamper, dash and rickety

Tattoo of driven metals, spent and cooling.

GREEN LANES

for Willis

We walked together, the hidden way,

Where once a line was

Lost, and found

Ourselves, as might have been

Expected, in the lap of Muswell

Hill, across the prime meridian.

We could perhaps remember

Walking so as reclamation, trespass

In the name of salvage, taking back

The commons, as I often said, more

In earnest than might otherwise

Be gleaned from my habitual

                  flippancy; however,

In the sun that paid us court

That day as though decanted

From many a summer's storage

In blind caves abandoned

Even by the pipistrelle, we felt

More akin to chosen

                  antiquarians,

Coming upon lost cupolas and spires

By happy chance, with lighting fit

For the occasion and no end

           of field and forest

               birds, translated

From the pens of Harringay and Palmer's

Green, effusive

In their praise (a blush of apricot

And sable indicating

No chaffinch, but the hoopoe, confidante

Of Solomon, or — talisman and sidekick

In assorted pranks and perils —

           the honeyguide, making

               north in search of sugar).

Although there was never much between

Me and the city, as the hoopoe flies,

Still, it took a tremble of surprise

To cross that border of dishevelled dock

And reticent, scuffed elders, to set foot

Upon a country

Where the red and silver buses ran

                              to time,

Where coffee could be had

For love or money

                       (usually

The latter, though we crossed

Our hearts and fingers all the same).

AVALON

Here is where they grow

Rust on a scale sufficient

To supply the country's

Needs for several

Centuries to come,

Mullein and nettles

High enough to hide

Their houses, gold

In the approximate

Shape of pears, wherever

Seed has fallen

Straight from giants'

Laughter into sunlight,

Into ready hands

Turned

Up and earth turned over.

QUARRY

Even the most clandestine

Tarns and lochans raise

A stint of glitter after

Rain, before the sun is all

Wrung out and hung to dry.

~

April, cascades in hand,

Allows a thought of May

     like morning waiting

For its moment in the mountains;

As for winter, keepsakes

And imitations play

             their part

In earnest, wavering

Away like surplus glass;

Brittle and brilliant, hard by the heart.

BERINGIA

i.

No visions of Dante, no versions of Rilke;

No Li Po, Mencius, nor Mandelstam; only
An attempt to paraphrase
A passage from Aquinas, but,
Faced with the potential
Energy of angels
You turned instead
To the next white, wordless spread —

The Arctic, islands and all
The unstaffed listening
Stations
To be found there, still.

ii.

These days, spring remains
A quibble, one end of an argument
In arguable humour, while
My feet swell

     at summer's least suggestion.

~

On at least one roof of the known world,
The impetus of bitumen has cooled,
Congealing to a schema of Siberian
Drainage basins — the Kolyma,
Amur and Indigirka ending
Where the sun has just begun
Reforming and bewildering
Magnolias from young,
Sanguine and univocal
Trees to hieroglyphs in disarray.

iii.

After the ice and iron

Ages, rust;

After the cables,

Cranes and derricks,

Earth and all your fill of dust.

SAXA LOQUUNTUR

With a name well and truly

Made by surveys at Isthmus,

Meticulous analysis of bull —

                leaping frescoes, Chenco

Grounds and knucklebones,

You joined the team unearthing

Strata of destruction

At Coogan's Bluff and Pigtown,

Sifting material

Remains from the Dark Age of Baseball.

~

Shielded from glare, you listen

As words play back

Against a moil of interference:

'Darkness', you insisted,

      'must be understood as a motif,

a metaphorical convention…

The game was surely played in sunlight …'

VENERATION

i.

Observed in transit, hooded,

Filtered, at the four

Points of contact, recto,

Verso, flat and tapered —

                    liable to hail

And storm, high pressure

Systems keeping weather

Lidded for a season, until grasses parch

Beyond the wit of rain or autumn to rescind

ii.

Stones in their pseudonyms and silver,

Sifting rock and light, the very dream

I want to walk right into, finding

Seeds and fossil

Barley on the moon, impressions

Made by tails of jays and wounded

Wrynecks on the little

Stones where weathers press

Close to the steppes of Venus,

All too apt to be mistaken

For corollaries of turbulence,

Symptoms of the season gathering

A head of steam and nothing more

FAIR ISLE TO YELL

You saw hands moving, catching
Not a word on the wind's account,
Numbered terns until you could
No longer vouch for the integrities
Of blue and blank and blinding white.

Each draws upon their own
Appraisal of the sea, their style
Unmistakeable despite
Iterated launderings, difference
In dye and warp and weather undergone;

No two boats, no gestures
Quite the same; stern or bearing
Betrays each complement
And every time, whatever flag
Runs for convenience, however

Many knots are made across

The skin of water; muffle oars

And engines all you want,

Damp the least lisp from the sails,

Someone always gives the herring

Gull the wink and sooner than

You think, sooner than you can

Say knife the whole

Wide world and all

The neighbours know the story.

MERE FRUITS

after a spell

on land, sea creatures

everywhere —

woodlice and americas,

as per the current

distributions;

cauliflowers

squat in frills and scuttles;

books, their spines

stove in, all skulk and flounder;

pepperpots, a touch of syzygy

gone to their heads,

lift and bustle

for the brightest

light, the nearest sign or portent

PRAXILLA'S RETURN

Despite the harvest mice and hornets going on

And on about their ideal home

Displays, their paperwork,

This is a quiet valley, altogether

Lush and lucky country:

                arbutus giving way without

Demur to thyme, cucumbers next

In line after the sun and moon and ocean-

                  explicating stars, pears, several

Families of fennel,

Furrows and at last

A farmer sowing

Salt, reminder of the cities,

How they used to grow and harvest here.

VIA NEGATIVA

show your hand

empty, all the rest

fleshed out in certain colours;

five bars, five denials

to the sun's impress

give away an hour

spent with clay,

time taking shape

against the rock,

through iron, burnt

bone and sienna,

stippled lime and umber;

ochre smudges, slurs

bright mouths, bold tongues;

if once they found, they have

forgotten, if they ever

held they lost, unnoticed,

registers of stone and winter;

　　　　whatever voice was

there, however summer

sounded to you, through

you we will see,

hear or imagine only

by your hand, telling

how it is

without you now

KUGAMI

Bones and stems, unprecedented

Weather for these parts;

Eulalia and bleached rush

Scamper,

Fling and flourish;

Wind up

From the south, delayed

By islands, sands

And oceans,

Breathes

A hasty kiss

Farewell, as if

To dispel a last,

Loitering

Thought, a shred of ash.

ALGEBRA

[Arab. *aljebr* reunion of broken parts
(*jabara* reunite), bone-setting]

al-jebr, reunion of distracted bone,

spilled stars on green and narrow sea;

as you said, Merwin, let it be —

marks of logic, mathematics

mapping

a zodiac in negative, uncounted

nicks and secrets of the skeleton

key, mantra or mandala

whispered in sand until a city rings

true, all song and shadow and no strings

MODES OF PRODUCTION

Outside, some chewing lichen, taking heart,

Spitting on their hands to get a head

Start on the task of marking, leaving

Something new and beautiful, once and for all,

Working with steady light and shadow on the wall.

Inside, despite the stray, dissimulated

Sway and exile of the sun

Among the younger lamps and fires,

We could tell burned from burnished

Thread, hawk moths from harvestmen,

The lie and limits of the land

From one another, truth

From what the wise and wealthy

Of this world would have us know.

SITTING DOWN WITH THE REGIME

i.

                    Time, we're told,

Before the clocks

Get rusty or the iron ends

                          up cold

And obsolete, to sit

Down with the regime, take

Scissors to the map, and shake.

ii.

Some say it was not so, while others still

Maintain that when the Cheyenne

Women found his body,

Unmistakeable in golden

                      hair and gaudy

Braid, they took an awl

To each ear, to make the point

That he could surely not have heard

Too good, or otherwise he spurned

Warnings given to him plain and clear

In words and ashes, when he went

South and sat with them below the arrows,

Smoking for peace beside Sweetwater River.

WINTER COUNT

i.

So this is how five months go by, then
Six all of a sudden; dry
Spells and reminders
Written in the clouds and roads, the many
Weeds and pebbles I must pick to weigh
Myself against a litany of winds at play;

At first, a year gone just a flinch
Too far to turn around
Again, I sat on cold and level
Stone, all ears for laughter, summons,
Explanation and the echo,
Distracted from the task
Of harvesting and holding on
To light in short
Rations of illumination
Released by January to London,

Watching iron creep

Like evening into each square inch of sky, aware,

Despite the wings and silver linings, that

As yet no joy would come,

Nor question find relief from seeking you up there;

Now, I gather unenthusiastic

Knees beneath me,

Crouch against a church, see only

Green in every field of vision, hear

Hawks and whispers in their wooden

Hideaways, and find myself beginning

To wonder if we ever really made it

Here as children, thinking nothing

Of the fact, transferring epitaphs

To narrow feint, much as summer makes a swallow

From blinks of rust and bronze, coordinates to follow.

ii.

February, still learning how to read

Between the lines and repetitions,

Whale-oil lamps and shadows of a century

Before the last:

        the declaration and destruction

Of republics; first and jubilant and final, fatal

Days of the Commune; bloody weeks and winters

Like no other; treaties made, no sooner

Broken; mountains

Hammered to the nub

        (as advertised

        in China), cradled,

Sifted and erupted out of California to the last,

Warped and muddy glint (while nations

Who had lived there as the gold had grown

        underfoot or underwater

Were cut down without stint and without quarter);

Railroads going everywhere and leaving

Some rich, more buried and their tracks

Behind; empires growing hand in hand

With fire and sword and famine, steam

Power, printed cottons, tea and stronger

Nostrums, some for home, some strictly

Kept for overseas consumption; Karl Marx,

Intimate as woodworm with the British

Museum Reading Room —

     seat G7, section AA,

As legend has it — gnawing

Cigars down to the tooth, resorting to the knife,

Creosote and opium and arsenic

For boils and a liver

Going south; Lone Dog in spirals

Marking years of peace and falling

Stars on skin (pipes

Passed around and blankets handed

Out as per the Treaties of Horse Creek,

Or Laramie, and Medicine Lodge); massacre,

Revolt and open war and men in sombre

Coats returning, regular as cold

Weather on the heels of autumn.

iii.

November rains, though not on paper;

Books still blank and baled, locked

Rooms filled with ink or windows

Misted to a steady Arctic

Grain, collecting

Charcoal ridge by ridge, defiles

White as if immune to writing.

With such reams and gatherings

For company, how could you ever

Keep your hands or sentences

In sequence, seventy-

                  five lines of verse

Translated daily in accordance

With prescription, eight or eighteen

                  hundred cigarettes

A day in any kind of order?

                Order,

Process and reason, rhyme

Or purpose, putting a shoulder

To the world and pushing,

To improve it or at least

Somehow to move it —

all of the above,

Perhaps you'll say (perhaps

I hear my own submerged, translated

Inclinations piping up), is neither

Yours nor any of your neighbours'

Business; ash and silver

Birches, oak and hemlock seem

To grow, while cuckoos carry on

Their usurpations all along

The lower reaches, where the rivers

Disappear from Scythia in rushes,

Whether or not you notice

and before even the sea

gets to the bottom of it ...

~

All that is said and done and sure

As day and diffidence will follow night;

Nevertheless, for this

One time we might

Set one of the smaller wheels

Rolling and roll with it, out of sight.

iv.

After winter, springs

Begin to hint at other things

Beside themselves, beyond the point

Where glass exasperates and metal sings;

I still look up when engines

Swoop and sputter or when trees

Renounce the world and lavish

Their share of tinsel on the breeze,

Still look to fields of flax and fodder

Crops, used as mirrors by the moon, in case

The least suspicion of your flight perturbs

Their placid moods, and find

The sun instead, ebullient and eager to get started

On a much anticipated comeback tour,

Designed to magic every zenith,

Beam and bow and leave

Us wanting more,

                wide-eyed and open-hearted.

ROLAND GARROS

I do not remember now if ever
I thought in honesty they played
At the pleasure of the desert, oaths
Taken in the teeth of the Simoom, wary

Lest they tread on scorpions, alert
For premonitions of a river,
Murmurs growing into spates,
Enough to carry
Nets and courts and crowds
Clean down the wadi and away;

Despite the trappings of the court, adherence
To the strictures of a feudal etiquette,
Service and return, sometimes
A Jacobin from the dais raised
A voice, insistent that at least
One precept of the revolution
Be observed, and so,

before the grass,

For two swift weeks, *égalité*

Held undivided sway

Over this empty quarter cut from clay.

Footnotes to the Small Hours

i.

under the moon's thumb, a remainder;

lees of night allow

a dream of trams, their tracks

yet legible despite

four decades and a fraction

more of disuse, reclamation,

overwriting, thoroughgoing

policies of pedestrianization;

mazing over brickwork's herringbone,

across the zebra crossings, errant

courses of a restless water,

a river in several minds,

each turn of humour

marked by diminutions

in the landscape's yield —

a wrinkled hill,

a ruined farm, a thwarted field

ii.

rope stands in the sky, at the accustomed station;

passing, a moon

takes hold and hauls

herself and all her scythes aloft

quickened metre after metre, she remembers

the mute and pensioned river as a mere

slip of a thing, a svelte tongue

feeling for sticklebacks

in awkward and deliberate dabs and scurries,

when running sure

had yet to settle as a second nature to her

iii.

our moon climbs further and remembers more —

how young mountains cut their teeth

on blimps and weather

balloons, hampering transhemispheric

flights until their fangs were fledged,

enamelled with moraine and scree,

grimy pelts of ice

like mildew on abandoned stooks

iv.

moonrise whets the tramlines to a slather:

insistent blades, each

following the scars

of water, followed by unerring,

faithful symptoms — standpipes, dowsers'

tents and faucets,

seeps and the mercurial

stage whisper, somewhere

between a tremor and a sound,

made by a certain mass of silver,

turning the matter over underground

Notes

[*Fayyum*]

Al Fayyum, or Faiyum, in Lower Egypt, is built on the site of
the ancient city of Crocodilopolis. The Faiyum Basin is home to
a distinctive tradition of sarcophagi, adorned with highly real-
istic encaustic facial portraits of the dead, which the desert climate has preserved almost without corruption.

Koiné ('common'), a form of Greek which drew on the various
vernaculars of the eastern Mediterranean, constituted a *lingua
franca* in the early years of the Common Era. It is the language
in which the New Testament is written.

The Hyksos were a dynasty, and perhaps an ethnic group from
the Levant or further east, who ruled Egypt in the Second In-
termediate Period, between the Middle and New Kingdoms,
from c.1800-1550 BCE. The Hellenistic Jewish historian
Josephus considered the 'Hyksos' to be the sons of Jacob, in-
vited to Egypt by their brother Joseph while famine raged in
Canaan.

[*Pilot*]

This poem is largely based on accounts of the trade between
the Greco-Roman world and the kingdoms of the Indian litto-
ral and Sri Lanka, as found in documents such as the *Periplus
of the Erythraean Sea* and Tamil poetry, which refers to the
Yavana (Greeks), who, after trading their wares, sailed away in
ships laden with pepper. *Malabathrum* was the name given by
the Romans to the leaves of various trees of the cinnamon family, gathered in Malabar and the Himalayas.

[*Goodnight-Loving Trail*]

In 1866, cowboys Charles Goodnight and Oliver Loving established a new cattle trail running north from Texas, to supply native American reservations, Rocky mountain mining camps, and the crews working on the Transcontinental Railroad. When Loving died of wounds sustained during a skirmish with Comanches, Goodnight fashioned a coffin from tin cans and drove his body home to Texas.

[*Gazetteer*]

Odontotyrannus (tyrannical tooth), is a name found in ancient Greek literature on India, and most probably refers to the rhinoceros; *fastitocalon*, or *aspidochelone* is a vast sea creature described in classical and mediaeval bestiaries and the Old English poem *The Whale*, fond of luring sailors onto its back, which they take for land, before plunging into the depths of the ocean.

[*Mannahatta*]

The Fresh Kills landfill site, on Staten Island, was opened in 1947 and eventually became one of the largest human structures on the face of the Earth, extending over 2,200 acres and rising higher than the Statue of Liberty. Closed in March 2001, the site was partially reopened after September 11 as a sorting-ground for debris from Ground Zero.

[*Looking Glass*]

The words in quotation marks paraphrase those of the folklor-
ist and historian Roger Welsch, in Ken Burns' PBS documen-
tary *The West* (Episode 5, 'The Grandest Enterprise Under
God').

[*Orlebar Variations*]

Chingkanshan, or Jinggang mountain, was home to large sec-
tions of the Chinese Communist Party, and site of the forma-
tion of the Red Army following the Shanghai massacre of 1927,
in which the Party's urban membership was decimated.
Gourds (but little else) grew plentifully at Chingkanshan, and
the lantern which I saw from a train window while immersed
in Edgar Snow's *Red Star Over China* (an account of the time
he spent with the Red Army in Yan'an, shortly after the Long
March) may well have been emblazoned with the popular
Chingkanshan slogan, 'down with capitalism, eat squash!'

Charnia, named after the Charnwood Forest in Leicestershire,
where their fossils were first identified, is a genus of Precam-
brian fractal organisms, with a fern-like appearance, and one of
the oldest known lifeforms on the planet.

[*Clippings*]

ταν αχειμαντον τε Μεμφιν και δονακωδεα Νειλον:
'Memphis spared by snow,/And the reedy Nile'. Bacchylides,
as translated here by Robert Fagles (*Bacchylides: The Complete
Poems* (Yale University Press, 1989, p.93)), extols the dry and
temperate Egyptian climate that has enabled papyrus fragments of his work, and that of other Greek lyric poets such as

Sappho, to survive, while elsewhere they have been consumed by damp.

[*Saxa Loquuntur*]

Pigtown was the local name for a patch of derelict land, frequented by hogs, on which, in 1909, Charles Ebbets began construction of the stadium which would be home to the Brooklyn Dodgers from 1913 until they moved to Los Angeles in 1958; Coogan's Bluff is an elevation behind the Polo Grounds in Upper Manhattan, home of the New York Giants until they decamped to San Francisco, also in 1958. Fans without tickets could watch games for free from the high ground.

Chenco was the name used in Appalachia for a game played at the city of Cahokia, centre of the mediaeval Mississippian culture, in the American Bottom Country of present-day Illinois; the game involved chasing and throwing spears at rolling discs of stone. Failure in the game was a cause of severe humiliation, and frequently led to suicide. Cf. Timothy R. Pauketat, *Ancient Cahokia and the Mississippians* (Cambridge University Press, 2004).

[*Praxilla's Return*]

The Greek poet Praxilla, who lived in the 5th century BCE, was the butt of frequent ridicule (not without a touch of misogyny) in ancient literary criticism, for her delight in apples, pears, and cucumbers, which she considered almost as beautiful as sunlight. For translations of the fragments of Praxilla's poetry, cf. Willis Barnstone, *Ancient Greek Lyrics* (4th Edition; Indiana University Press, 2010), p.154.

[*Kugami*]

The translation from Ryōkan is by Burton Watson; cf. *Ryōkan: Zen Monk-Poet of Japan* (Columbia University Press, 1977), p.61.

[*Sitting Down with the Regime*]

In November 1868, George Custer and the US Seventh Cavalry launched a surprise attack against an encampment of the Southern Cheyenne chief Black Kettle, on the Washita River in Oklahoma. Black Kettle, who had survived a previous massacre by white troops at Sand Creek in Colorado in 1864, was killed in the fighting. During negotiations which followed the winter campaign, Custer smoked a pipe of peace with the chief Rock Forehead at Sweetwater Creek, while seated beneath the sacred arrows of the Southern Cheyenne. Doubtful of promises of peace if the Cheyenne remained on reservations designated by the US government, Rock Forehead tapped out the ashes of the pipe on Custer's boots, and warned him that if he broke his promise, the Everywhere Spirit would ensure that his death followed soon after.

Custer was killed at the Battle of the Little Bighorn, where he had once again launched a surprise attack, against an encampment of Cheyenne and Lakota; reports vary as to the treatment of his body, with many insisting that it was deliberately left untouched, while others recount the legend that two Cheyenne women pierced his ears with sewing awls to improve his hearing. Reports of the mutilation of corpses, which was intermittently practised by both native American and US troops, had of course long been a staple ingredient in white condemnation of Indian 'savagery'.

More poetry from *Starborn* Poets...

Alex Barr:
>   *Henry's Bridge*
>   *Letting in the Carnival (published by Peterloo)*

Ann Byrne-Sutton:
>   *High June*
> . *Come Back to Avalon*

Phil Malleson:
>   *Poems*

Paul Steffan Jones:
>   *Lull of the Bull*
>   *The Trigger-Happiness*

Peter Oram:
>   *White*
>   *Tease it Free*
>   *Revolver Night (with Diane Walkey)*
>   Translations:
>>   From the French cycles of poems of R.M.Rilke:
>>>   *Valaisian Quatrains*
>>>   *Orchards*
>>>   *Roses*
>>   From the Russian of the poets of the 'Silver Age':
>>>   *The Page and the Fire (by Arc Publications)*